890 09

MEDICINE IN THE FUTURE

Mark Lambert

The Bookwright Press
New York · 1986

Tomorrow's World

Our Future in Space
The Telecommunications Revolution
Lasers in Action
The Robot Age
Living in the Future
Future Sources of Energy
Transportation in the Future
The Future for the Environment
Medicine in the Future

First published in the United States in 1986 by
The Bookwright Press
387 Park Avenue South
New York, NY 10016

First published in 1986 by Wayland (Publishers) Limited
61 Western Road, Hove, East Sussex, England, BN3 1JD

© Copyright 1986 Wayland (Publishers) Limited

ISBN 0–531–18078–6
Library of Congress Catalog Card Number: 85–73671

Phototypset by Kalligraphics Ltd., Redhill, Surrey
Printed in Italy by G. Canale & C.S.p.A., Turin

Contents

Machines and medicine   4

Computers in medicine   11

Surgery in tomorrow's world   16

The fight against disease   27

People and medicine   35

Glossary   46
Further reading   46
Index   47

Machines and medicine

Medicine today is concerned with the diagnosis, cure and prevention of disease. As in many other aspects of human life, technology has begun to play an increasingly important part in the fight against disease. Many machines, such as kidney machines, heart-lung machines and life support units, are now essential features of a well equipped hospital. In the future, we can expect to see an increasing range of machines used to diagnose and treat people's illnesses.

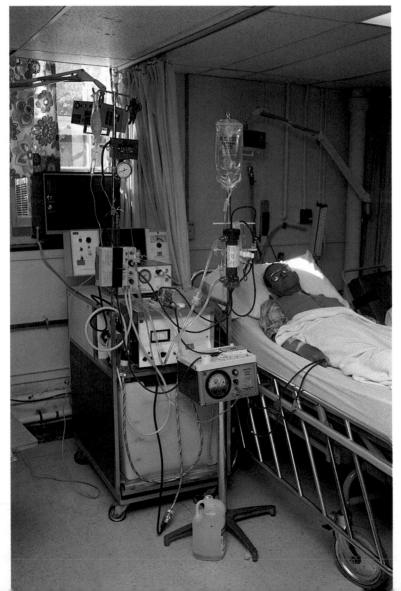

A kidney machine removes waste materials from the blood when a patient's kidneys fail to function properly.

An endoscope allows the surgeon to examine internal organs without performing surgery. A view of a healthy stomach, showing the opening into the intestine.

Looking inside the body

Until recently, the only way for doctors to examine the inner parts of a patient's body was to perform surgery. Advances in technology, however, have now made it possible to study the body's inner organs using only very minor surgery. Some machines can be used without harming the patient's body in any way.

Among the most useful modern instruments are endoscopes. These enable doctors to examine the interior of the body, usually through a natural body opening, by inserting a lighted optical tube into the cavity. An endoscope contains bundles of fine glass fibers, along which light can be transmitted regardless of how much the fibers are bent. There are at least two bundles of these fibers. One transmits light to illuminate the organ being examined deep inside the body. The other has a lens at the end, which carries light from the organ to an eyepiece.

In addition to the bundles of optical fibers, the shaft of an endoscope carries various tubes and wires. An air pipe

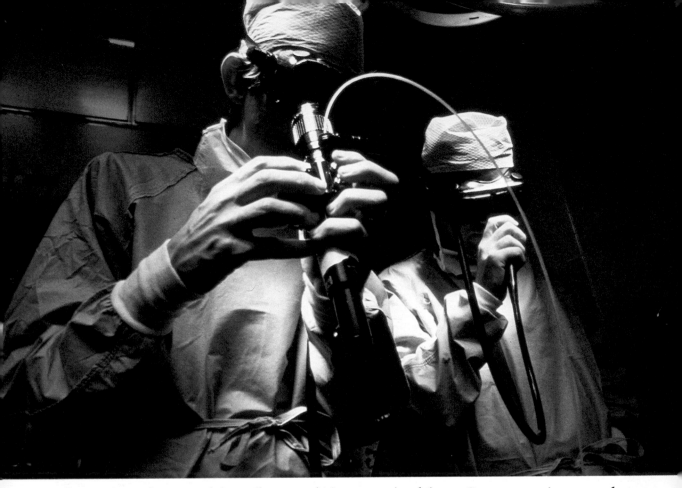

allows air to be passed into the area being examined in order to inflate it, making the examination easier. Another pipe can suck out liquids, and there are wires to control the direction in which the tip of the endoscope points. These are operated by controls near the eyepiece.

Endoscopes are often used to diagnose illness. They can be used to examine the insides of many body cavities, such as the stomach, intestines, womb, nose and even joints. Equipped with the right tools, such as forceps and scissors, they can be used to remove tissue for testing. They can even perform small operations, such as the removal of unwanted growths on the wall of the intestine, or the removal of gallstones. Using a powerful laser, it is possible to stop internal bleeding by sealing off the broken blood vessels. In the future, more endoscope operations will become possible, thus doing away with the need for major surgery in a number of cases.

Surgeons using an endoscope and a laser to seal broken blood vessels during an operation.

Scanning the body

An endoscope is inserted into the body. However, there are a variety of machines that can be used to examine the body without penetrating any tissues. A thermal imager can be used to detect "hot spots" in the body which indicate abnormal growth. Thermography, a form of photography using film sensitive to infrared (heat) rays, can detect tumors and cysts at an early stage.

There are also several types of scanning machines. The oldest of these is the Computerized Axial Tomography (CAT) scanner. This uses a form of radiation known as X rays. As with an ordinary X-ray machine, the scanner works on the principle that different tissues absorb different amounts of X rays. The varying amounts of X rays that remain unabsorbed by the body as the beam passes through are recorded on film as a picture. Unlike a conventional X-ray machine, the CAT scanner measures the radiation absorbed by a "slice" or cross-section of the body. The information is passed to a computer, which creates a

Heat from organs of the body is recorded on film sensitive to infrared or heat rays. In this way, attention can be drawn to areas where the levels of heat are abnormally high or low.

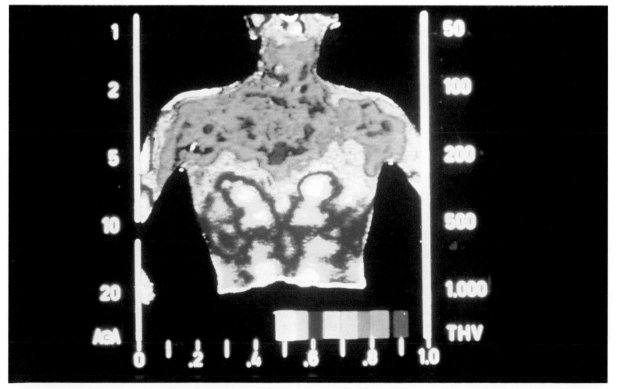

7

picture of the "slice." To examine an organ thoroughly several "slices" are recorded.

A CAT scanner subjects the body to far less radiation than a conventional X-ray machine. But X rays are harmful, and for some purposes, such as studying unborn babies, they are never used. An ultrasound scanner, however, has no harmful effects. This machine produces high-frequency sound waves – too high for humans to hear – that are reflected at places where one tissue stops and another begins. Ultrasound scanners are best known for their use in studying babies in their mothers' wombs, but they can also be used to detect problems in such organs as the kidneys, pancreas and eye, and to study how the heart is working.

This shows a CAT scan of the skull with an inset of the machine itself.

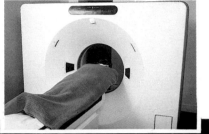

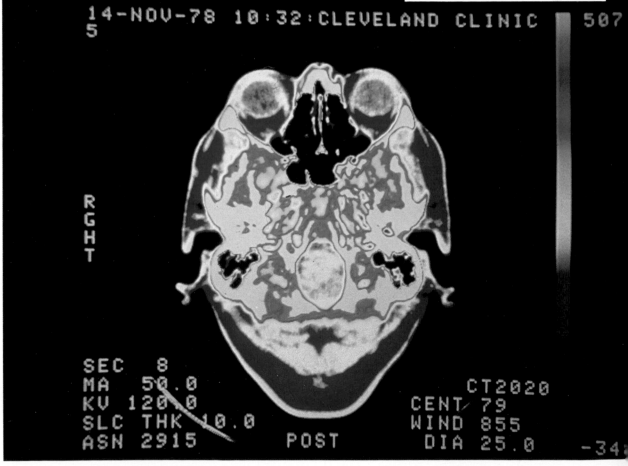

14-NOV-78 10:32:CLEVELAND CLINIC 507
5

RGHT

SEC 8
MA 50.0
KV 120.0
SLC THK 10.0
ASN 2915   POST

CT2020
CENT 79
WIND 855
DIA 25.0   -34

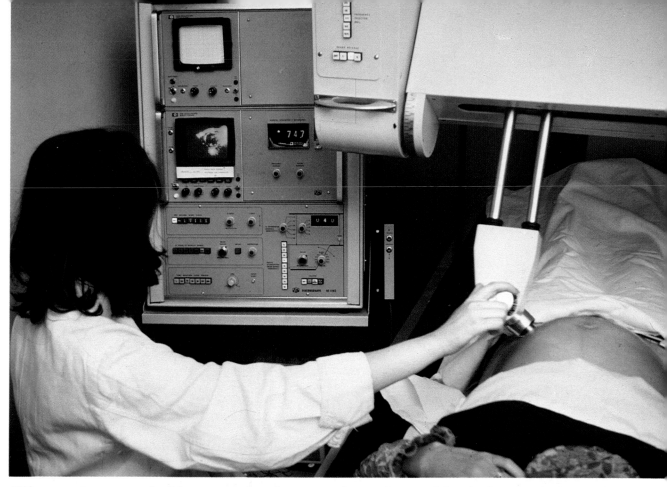

Ultrasound scanners build up a picture of an internal organ or developing fetus from soundwaves reflected from the different tissues.

Another type of scanning machine is the gamma camera. Chemicals that are radioactive are injected into the body, and collect in the organ under examination. The camera picks up gamma radiation from these chemicals and records a picture of those that have collected in the organ. Bone scans to detect cancer are also commonly done in this way, but other organs that can be examined include the brain, lungs, liver and a number of glands. The filtering action of the kidneys and the flow of blood through the arteries can also be studied in this way, by taking a series of pictures and processing them in a computer.

The most recent type of scanner is known as the Positron Emission Tomography (PET) scanner. This machine is much more versatile than the CAT scanner. It can be used to detect tumors in the brain, show damage due to a stroke, and even show which parts of the brain are most active at

any particular time. Finally, one of the latest machines is the Nuclear Magnetic Resonance Imager (NMR), which is used to study the distribution of certain atoms in the body. Abnormal concentrations of atoms may indicate disease.

The Nuclear Magnetic Resonance Imager measures the concentration of certain atoms in the body.

Computers in medicine

A computer is a vital part of any scanning machine. But in medicine, as in many other aspects of modern life, computers are used for a wide range of tasks.

For example, computers are used in radiotherapy treatment for cancer. Radiotherapy works on the basis that if body tissues exposed to radiation absorb enough of it cells will be injured or even destroyed. In the case of cancerous (malignant) cells this is an ideal form of treatment. Unfortunately, radiation does not selectively destroy cancer cells; it damages all cells, normal and malignant, by which it is absorbed. Success of such treatment depends upon the ability of the normal cells to regenerate following radiation

A doctor studies a computerized image of the area of the body under examination by a CAT scanner.

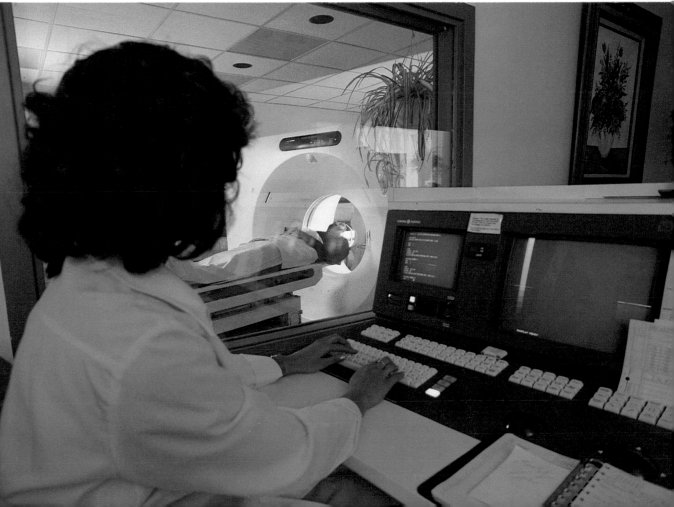

injuries. As the treatment progresses, the computer monitors the radiation dosage received by different parts of the body. This helps the radiotherapist to deliver the maximum possible dose to the cancer growth while reducing the damage to the surrounding tissues to a minumum. Computers are also used to monitor many of the body functions of patients, particularly in intensive care units. One computer can monitor several patients at the same time.

A computer is an essential part of a hospital intensive care unit.

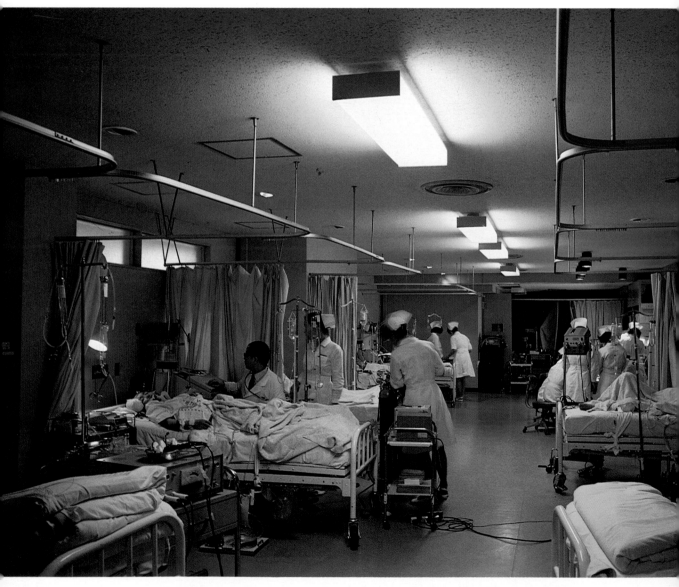

Patients' records can be stored on computer, providing swift and easy access.

Another important use for computers is in storing information. Computer data banks are used in clinical laboratories and many doctors are beginning to store people's medical records on computers. In the future it should be possible to link doctors' computers with hospital computers in local area networks. This will enable doctors to find out what they need to know about a patient quickly – particularly important in an emergency. Research into how, where and why diseases occur will also be made easier. There will, of course, have to be safeguards to keep personal medical data from falling into the wrong hands.

Computers can also be used in the training of doctors. Some programs test the ability of students to diagnose illness by presenting them with "symptoms" and asking questions. Other programs pretend to be living systems, which "respond" when drugs or anaesthetics are "given," thus testing the students' ability to prescribe the right treatment.

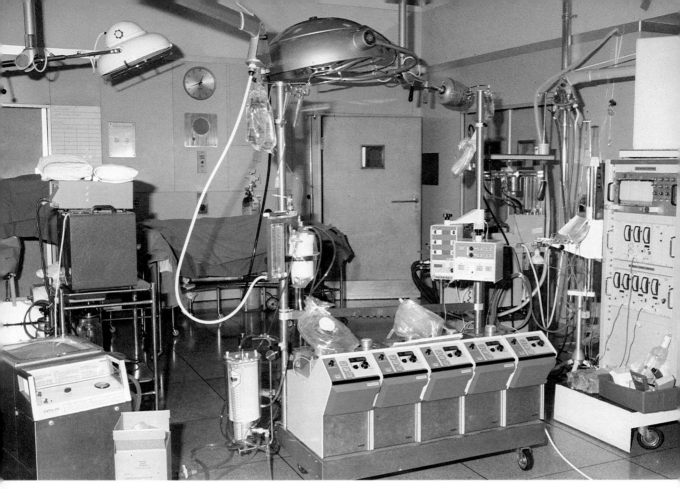

The heart-lung machine (center) keeps the body alive during heart surgery.

In addition, research is being carried out into the use of computers for diagnosis. Programs known as "expert systems" have been devised to help doctors work out what is wrong with patients from the symptoms they describe. There are even programs that allow a patient to "talk" directly with the computer itself (by means of push buttons). It has been found that many patients are more willing to give frank answers to a computer than to a human doctor.

Supporting life

Many people alive today owe their lives to the machines of an intensive care unit and the people who operate them. Critically ill patients who would have died quickly can now be restored to health thanks to modern technology.

Among the most important machines in an intensive care unit are respirator. Critically ill patients are often unable to breathe, and these machines keep air moving in and out of their lungs. A modern respirator electronically controls the pressure, flow and time of each breath, together with the amounts of oxygen, nitrogen and carbon dioxide. The air is supplied to the patient via a tube through the mouth, nose or (in the case of long-term patients) through the neck.

Patients are also linked to a number of different monitors. Breathing is monitored by devices that measure oxygen and acid levels in the blood. The activity of the heart is monitored by an electrocardiograph (ECG) and is shown on a video display. A cerebral function monitor (CFM) can be used to monitor a patient's brain activity. Temperature and blood pressure are also monitored. Food (in the form of glucose solution), salt solution and drugs are administered via drip feeds into the patient's veins.

In the future, intensive care units will undoubtedly continue to be improved and refined. At present it is not possible to take over the function of the heart (using a heart–lung machine) for more than a few hours – for example during heart surgery. But in future it may become possible to take over this and other functions of the body in order to sustain a patient's life. It will therefore be important to make sure that, in spite of all the computers and machines, hospitals remain places where people are cared for with dignity and humanity.

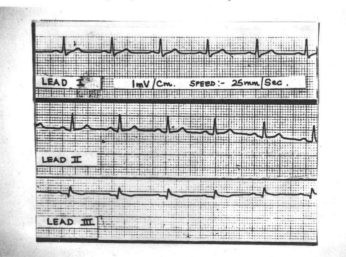

A normal electrocardiogram pattern.

Surgery in tomorrow's world

Two surgeons use an operating microscope to join blood vessels together.

Modern surgery can be said to have begun during the mid 1800s. Until then surgical operations had been rather primitive, performed without the use of anesthetics or antiseptics. During the 1500s and 1600s surgery was not even performed by doctors. Limbs were amputated by barber surgeons, whose main profession was cutting hair! Since the 1800s, however, surgical techniques have changed dramatically. Today it is possible to perform operations that once seemed impossible. Severed limbs can be sewn back on again and many organs of the body can be replaced by artificial parts.

Below *Until the 1840s there was no satisfactory method of anesthetizing the patient. This resulted in operations that were highly distressing both for the patient and the doctor.*

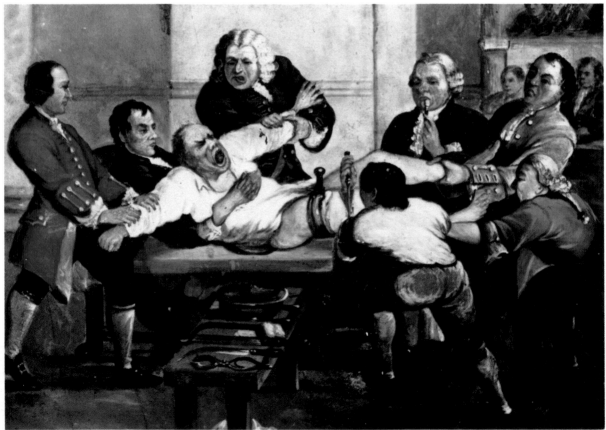

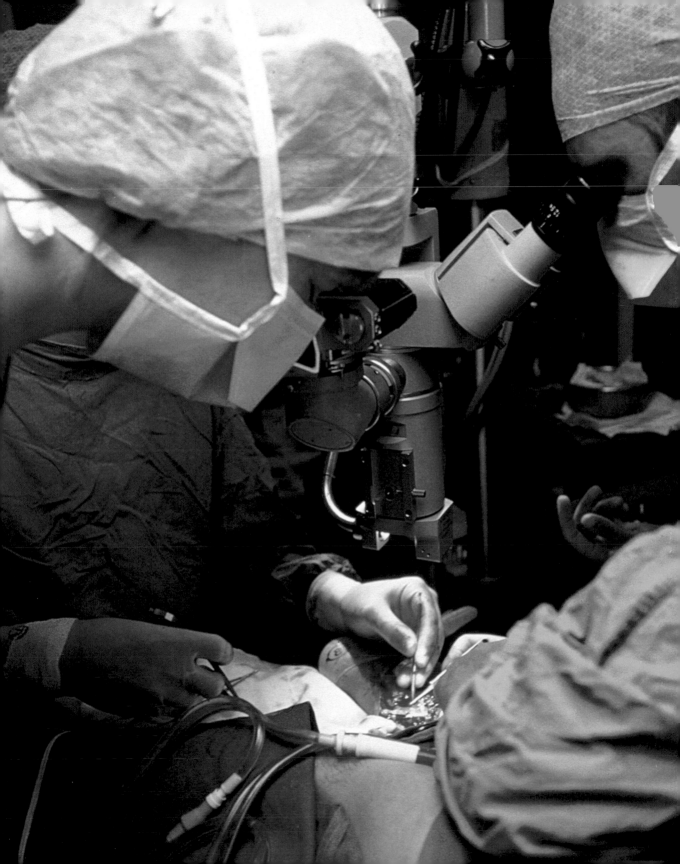

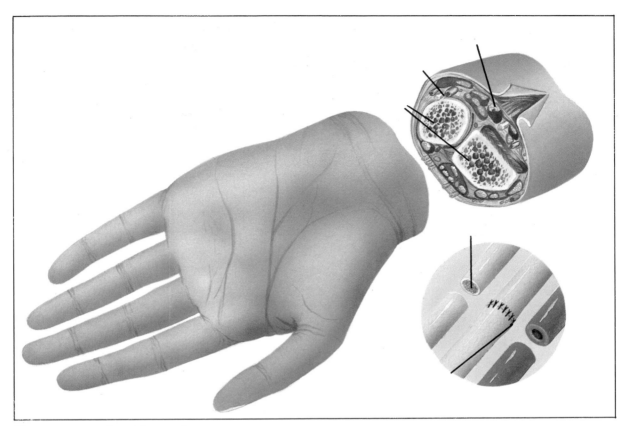

Surgery under the microscope

Thanks to the development of precision optical instruments and delicate miniature surgical instruments, surgeons can now operate on body structures that cannot even be seen clearly with the naked eye. Microsurgery has enabled surgeons to replace hands, feet, arms and legs that have been cleanly severed in accidents. Before the operation, the limb is cooled as quickly as possible to prolong its "life" – limb death occurs very quickly at room temperature. The surgeons carefully match up the severed tendons, blood vessels and nerves. Then slowly and painstakingly, using binocular microscopes, the surgeons join up the various parts. First the bones are pinned together. Then the major blood vessels and tendons are sewn together. The finest stitches are then used to join the nerves.

Microsurgery is also used to repair limbs that have been badly damaged, using bone and tissue from other parts of the body. Other operations that involve microsurgery

Severed limbs can be reattached to the body with the aid of micro-surgery.

18

include replacing a lost finger or thumb with a toe and inserting bypass arteries in patients who have had a stroke or are likely to have one. As the techniques of microsurgery are refined, many more operations will become possible.

Lasers and medicine

Among the most recently developed surgical techniques are those for operating on the body's most delicate and complicated organs, such as the eye and the brain. Surgery involving the use of lasers has made it possible to treat the finest tissues and blood vessels. A high powered laser beam is focused on the required point and just a quick burst of light is enough to burn away the diseased tissue.

A laser being used to remove birthmarks. Lasers can also perform very complicated operations on the eye and brain.

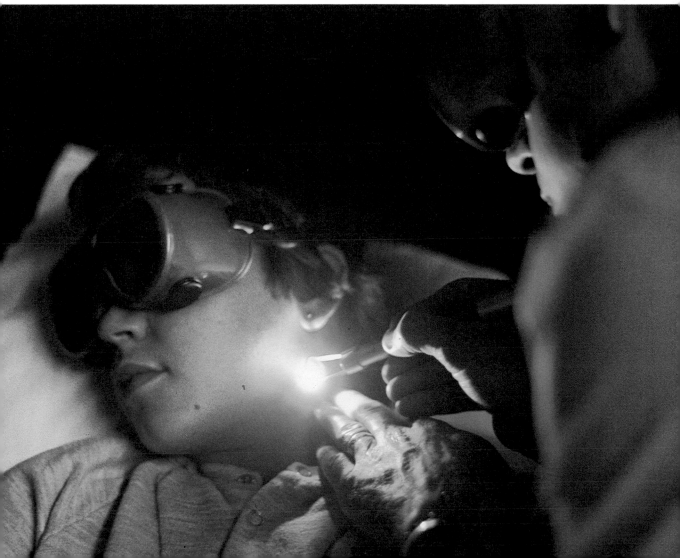

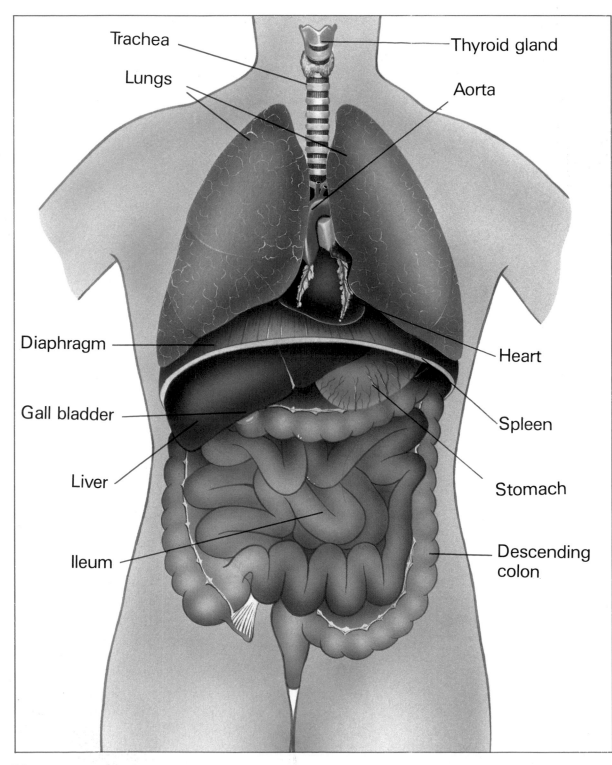

Trachea

Lungs

Diaphragm

Gall bladder

Liver

Ileum

Thyroid gland

Aorta

Heart

Spleen

Stomach

Descending colon

Lasers are used in other operations, for example , stomach operations, to remove diseased tissue and cauterize and seal broken blood vessels.

Surgeons can now cut open the brain to remove brain tumors and abscesses, both of which were once fatal. Minor brain damage caused by accidents can sometimes be repaired by surgery.

Brain surgery is one of the most difficult of all modern medical activities. For the future we cannot be certain how far techniques will progress, but much research is being done on how brain and nerve tissue grows and is repaired. Some progress is being made in the use of brain implants – inserting healthy tissue to replace damaged parts of the brain. At present this has only been done successfully in mice. But eventually it may become possible to treat diseases such as Parkinson's disease, and even some of the effects of old age by means of brain implants.

Transplant surgery

Transplant surgery is the process of taking a healthy organ from one person and using it to replace the diseased organ of another person. The first successful human transplants were done over thirty years ago. Today, kidney transplants are fairly routine. One advantage of this operation is that living donors can be used – a person can survive perfectly well with one kidney. Other organs must come from dead donors and this poses several problems. The organs have to be removed after the donor's brain has stopped working, but before the rest of the body has died. They have to be kept supplied with oxygen right up to the moment of removal and they must be kept in perfect condition before being inserted into the patient.

Today, increasing numbers of heart transplants are being performed and even small children are receiving new hearts. Other versions of this operation include the heart-lung transplant, in which the patient is given a complete set of heart and lungs, together with the blood vessels that connect them. In other cases the patient's own heart is left in place and an additional new heart is inserted in the right hand side of the chest.

Diagram of the body, showing internal organs.

21

One of the main problems in transplant surgery is that the system that normally defends the patient's body against infection recognizes the transplanted organ as "foreign" material, and starts to attack it – the so-called "rejection reaction." To reduce this possibility, doctors try to match the tissue types of the donor and receiver as closely as possible. Special drugs (immunosuppressive) can be used, which help to reduce this reaction of the body's defense system, but they must be used carefully. If the patient's defense system is lowered enough to tolerate "foreign material," there is a danger that it will also be unable to resist infections.

Recently, surgeons have begun to have some success in transplanting livers. In the future, transplants may also help people suffering from diabetes, a disease in which there is usually too much sugar in the blood. Normally, a hormone called insulin controls the sugar level. Insulin is produced by the pancreas, but occasionally this ceases to

Surgeons wear special gowns, which totally enclose their bodies. This ensures that the patient is operated on in a sterile atmosphere.

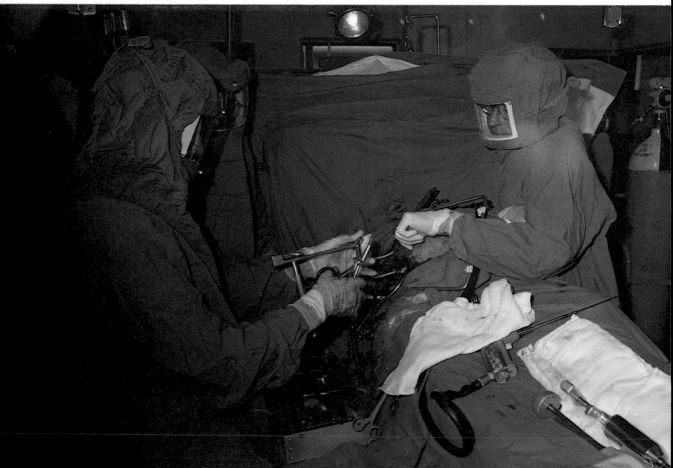

Open-heart surgery in progress.

function properly. Pancreas transplants have been tried, but most are rejected by the body's defense system. Another method is to transplant just the insulin-producing parts of the pancreas. The recent development of monoclonal antibodies has helped to reduce the chances of these insulin-producing parts being rejected. These are specially made substances which neutralize the cells that cause the rejection. They can also help to prevent the transplanted material from attacking the receiver's body defenses, which sometimes occurs in patients who have received bone marrow transplants.

In the future whole limb transplant could become possible. Until recently, such an idea has seemed to belong only in monster movies. But some researchers in California have had some success in transplanting the limbs of rats. The same scientists have shown that if young rabbits are given transplants of such things as ears, jaws or pieces of skull, the transplanted parts grow with their new owners.

Many parts of the body can now be replaced with artificial substitutes. The first crude artificial limbs were made in the 1500s. Modern artificial limbs are highly sophisticated devices and some work by picking up tiny electrical signals given off by the muscles that remain in the wearer's limb.

Bones, joints, arteries and veins can be replaced, using modern metals, plastics and other materials. One recently developed material is known as Bioglass. This is a ceramic material that actually forms a chemical bond with living material and should make artificial parts work better and last longer. Bioglass has been used to replace ear bones and the roots of extracted teeth. In the future it is hoped to make replacement hip joints using Bioglass.

In many patients, the heart's own natural pacemaker stops working properly. Such people can benefit from the use of artificial pacemakers, modern versions of which can

Modern artificial limbs have become more and more sophisticated. This little girl is able to use her left arm to perform quite complicated tasks.

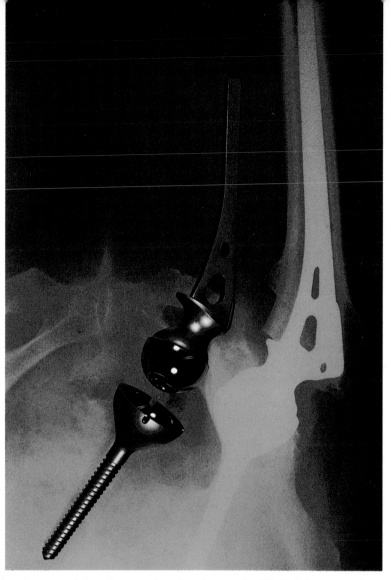

Scientists are researching suitable materials from which replacement joints, bones and arteries can be made. This hip joint is made from a very lightweight metal.

be inserted in the patient's chest. Artificial heart valves can be inserted into a patient's heart. Recently, scientists have devised completely artificial hearts, although as yet such hearts have to be powered by large machines outside the body and have not been shown to be successful for any length of time.

Another recent device is a "bionic ear," or cochlea implant, that can be used as a cure for some forms of deafness. The implant is inserted into the mastoid bone behind the patient's ear and is connected directly to the auditory (hearing) nerve. A microphone picks up the sound, which is converted into digital radio signals by a device

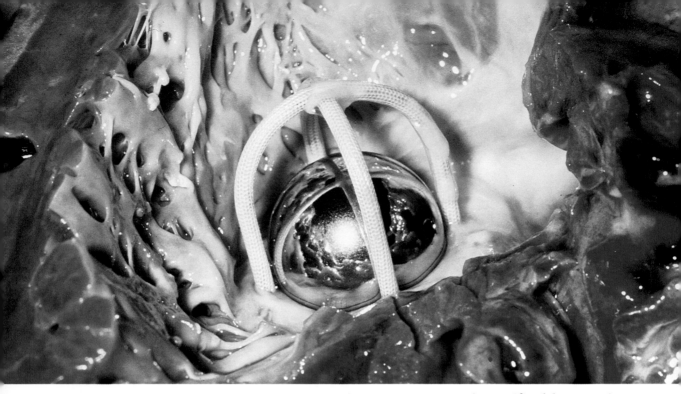

carried in the patient's pocket. The implant then picks up these radio signals and converts them into electrical signals.

An artifical heart valve is placed into the heart.

Spare part surgery has certain advantages over transplant surgery. There is less chance of rejection and the new organ cannot become diseased. And a donor does not have to be found. But in the near future the two forms of surgery are likely to complement each other. Research into how the body rejects transplanted organs will help in the development of new materials that biological tissues will accept.

In the long run there will probably be a limit to the number of organs that can successfully be replaced. There may be miniature artificial kidneys that can be implanted into the body (existing artificial kidneys are large machines), nuclear powered hearts and even artificial lungs. But some of the body's most complicated organs, such as the liver, may never be replaced. And in spite of the recent advances concerning brain implants, the use of artificial brains and brain transplants will remain in the realms of science fiction.

The fight against disease

In 1979, the World Health Organization (WHO) announced that smallpox, once one of the world's most dreaded killer diseases, had finally been wiped out. This remarkable achievement was the result of a worldwide campaign that lasted for many years. However, we are still left with many serious diseases, and new diseases may occasionally become a problem. Scientists are constantly searching for new ways of preventing and curing disease.

Preventing disease

One way of keeping people from developing a disease is to give a vaccine. A vaccine is made by taking the organism responsible for a disease and changing it slightly, so that it becomes harmless. If this modified organism is then introduced into the body (by injection or by mouth), the body's defense system reacts, producing antibodies (special proteins in the blood) to attack the invader. These antibodies, once produced, remain present in the blood and are able to combat any later invasion by the disease-causing organism. A vaccine therefore gives the body an immunity against a disease. Smallpox was wiped out by the worldwide use of cowpox vaccine, which causes the body to produce antibodies that neutralize both the relatively harmless cowpox virus and the killer smallpox virus. As a result of the vaccination program, everyone who came into contact with the smallpox virus was immune to it. And, as no virus can survive for long outside a living cell, the smallpox virus was wiped out.

Many other virus diseases can be prevented by vaccination. Examples include polio, yellow fever, whooping cough and measles. A wide range of bacterial diseases, such as diphtheria, cholera, tuberculosis, typhoid and tetanus, can also be prevented in this way. Among the latest vaccines are those that prevent meningitis and german measles, and there are improved vaccines against rabies and polio. Influenza (flu) vaccines are also now available and can save

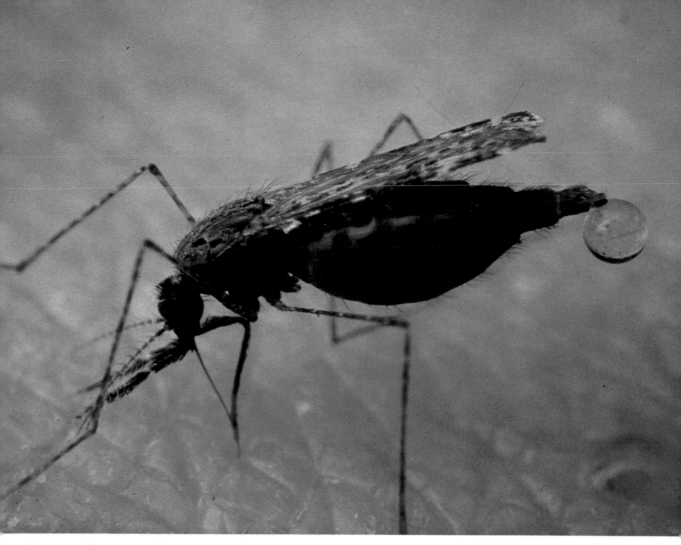

Above *Malaria remains one of the world's incurable diseases. It is caused by the bite of an infected mosquito.*

Large-scale vaccination programs are helping to wipe out world diseases.

the lives of elderly people and those prone to asthma and other illnesses connected with the lungs.

One of the most recently developed vaccines is the one that combats the hepatitis B virus, one of three (or maybe four) viruses that attack the liver. This vaccine was produced by genetic engineering, but recently an even more effective vaccine has been developed. Genetic engineers are also close to producing a vaccine against malaria, a killer disease caused by a tiny single celled animal parasite in tropical countries.

In the next ten years or so we may have vaccines against bilharzia (caused by a parasitic worm), sleeping sickness and rotavirus – a virus that causes diarrhea and may result in the death of young children. Finally, there is the prospect

29

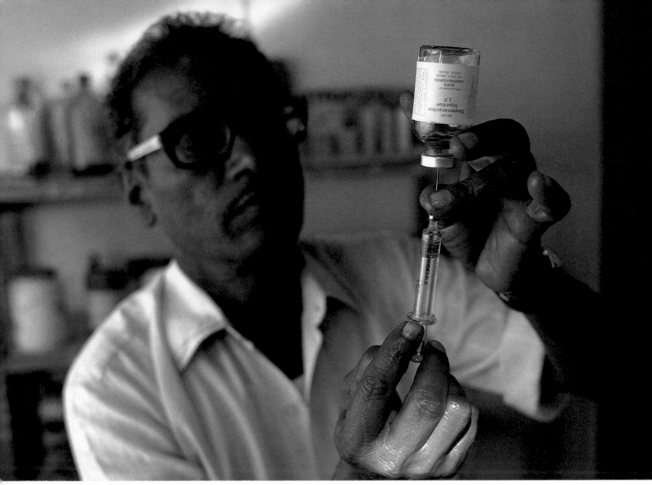

of producing vaccines against cancer. Scientists are already testing a vaccine that may be effective against a form of blood cancer known as Burkitt's lymphoma.

Curing disease

The antibiotic drug penicillin is produced by the fungus *Penicillium* and is poisonous to a wide range of disease-causing organisms. Since the discovery of penicillin in 1929 a number of other fungi have been shown to produce such "antibiotic" substances. However, the increasing use of antibiotics has resulted in the appearance of new strains of bacteria which can resist them. So scientists are constantly searching for new antibiotics. Seaweeds and other marine organisms have recently begun to yield antibiotics, and scientists have also started to alter artificially the structure of natural antibiotics so as to overcome the resistance of the bacteria.

Antibiotics such as Oxytetracycline can be injected into the body or taken in tablet form.

Modern medicine relies on the use of many drugs. In addition to antibiotics used to treat bacterial infections, there are drugs used to combat viruses, fungi and animal parasites. Most of the body's functions can be controlled by the use of drugs. Some of these drugs come from natural sources, others are made artificially.

New drugs are constantly being developed. One of the latest is known as interferon. This is a protein substance that the body produces naturally in minute amounts as it tries to defend itself against an invading virus. In 1980 scientists succeeded in creating an artificial source of this

Tiny capsules being filled with accurate amounts of antibiotic.

substance using genetic engineering. Even more recently, scientists have devised methods of producing interferon using yeast cells and human cancer cells. Interferon is now being produced in increasing amounts. It is effective against a wide range of viruses, including the killer Green Monkey virus and may be useful against the common cold virus. It has also been used to treat some forms of cancer.

Monoclonal antibodies are produced by combining antibody-producing cells with cancer cells to form hybrid cells. These multiply rapidly, increasing the supply of antibodies.

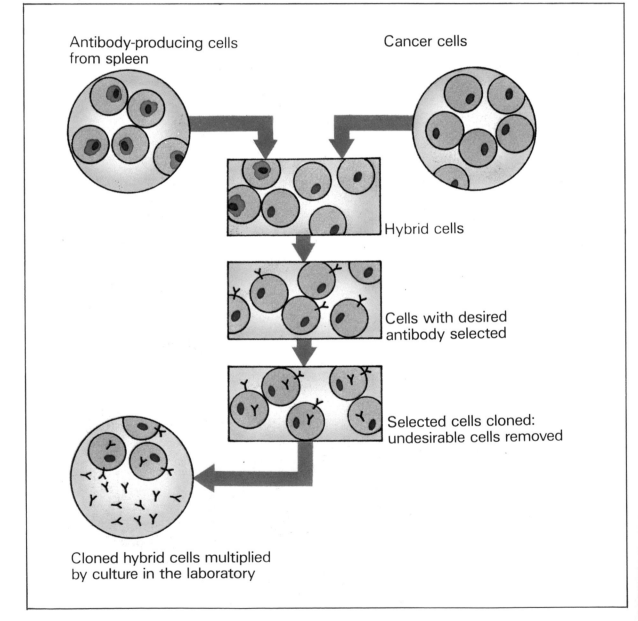

Antibody-producing cells from spleen

Cancer cells

Hybrid cells

Cells with desired antibody selected

Selected cells cloned: undesirable cells removed

Cloned hybrid cells multiplied by culture in the laboratory

This child is being treated for skin cancer. In the future, monoclonal antibodies could play a major part in curing this disease.

Among the most remarkable medical breakthroughs in recent times is the "invention" of monoclonal antibodies. These are very pure, concentrated forms of the antibodies that the human body normally produces in its fight against invading germs. Monoclonal antibodies, have the advantage that they are designed to attack only one specific foreign substance and have no side effects. They are produced by combining human spleen cells (which produce the antibodies) with cancer cells. The resulting hybrid cells have the ability of spleen cells to produce antibodies and the ability of cancer cells to multiply rapidly. Chemical means are then used to select the cells with the desired antibodies.

Monoclonal antibodies have a wide range of uses. If they

are injected into the body, they rapidly make their way to the site of the infection for which they are specific. By chemically attaching a radioactive substance to the antibodies, it is possible, using a gamma camera, to see if they accumulate at a particular site, and thus if a particular infection is present. Spina bifida in unborn babies, diabetes, hepatitis B and some forms of cancer can now be diagnosed in this way. Radioactive labeled monoclonal antibodies can also be used to show the extent of damage to heart muscle after a heart attack.

The treatment of cancer

Monoclonal antibodies can be used to help in matching tissues before organ transplants and in recognizing the first signs of rejection after a transplant. They can also be used to help produce very pure interferon, and in the future many other substances may be purified in the same way. One possibility for the future is in the treatment of cancer. Recently scientists have succeeded in attaching a poisonous substance to antibodies that only attack certain cancer cells. The antibodies carry the poison to the cancer site and the cancer cells are destroyed, leaving other cells unharmed.

Cancer is one of the world's most dreaded diseases. Some cancers can be controlled relatively easily, but there are many for which there are as yet no cures. At present, monoclonal antibodies remain the best hope for curing cancers in the future. Many other diseases remain to be overcome.

New diseases sometimes appear. A particularly deadly virus that has appeared in the last few years is human T-cell leukemia virus III (HTLV-III), which attacks certain cells in the body's immune system and allows normally rare infections to invade. The disease, commonly known as acquired immune deficiency syndrome (AIDS), is spreading and a great deal of research is being undertaken to find a cure.

People and medicine

Modern living conditions and health care enable people to live longer than ever before. The maximum age for a human remains about 120 years. Whereas once most people died between the ages of forty and sixty, today more and more people live into their seventies, eighties and nineties. Scientists are currently working on the chemistry of ageing. In the future, they hope to be able to counteract some of the effects of ageing and extend human life spans by at least another ten years.

Modern living conditions and health care enable people to live longer than ever before.

At the same time more and more children survive infancy. So the world's population is increasing. Currently there are about 4.7 billion people in the world and this figure is expected to increase to about 6 billion by the year 2000, and should stabilize at about 10 billion by the end of the next century. This in itself should not create medical problems. More people will undoubtedly need more hospitals and other medical facilities. But there will be correspondingly more people to tend the sick, and it is to be hoped that people will be less prone to disease as new cures and preventions are discovered.

Such cures and preventions are needed most in today's underdeveloped countries, where malnutrition and parasitic diseases are particularly common. Poor soil, lack of rain and poor hygiene contribute a great deal to disease in these Third World countries.

A medical helicopter equipped with an intensive care unit.

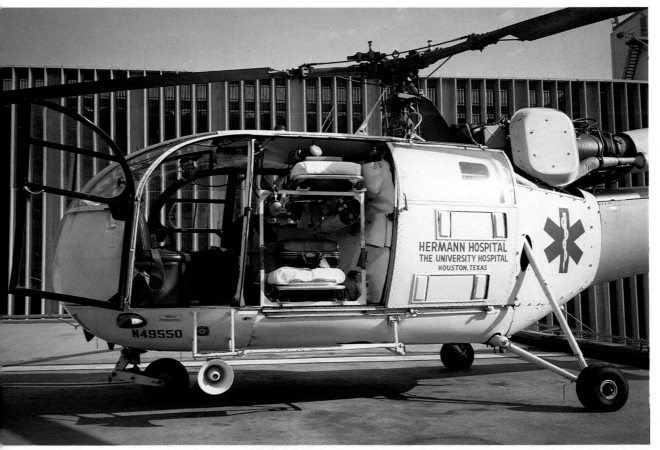

Poor housing and hygiene conditions contribute a great deal to disease.

Alternative medicine

Conventional medicine is based on a scientific approach to the human body. Knowledge of the body's structure and chemistry has enabled scientists and doctors to devise operations and drugs to control and cure diseases. When conventional medicine is unable to find a satisfactory treatment for prevailing health problems, such as backache, people frequently turn to alternative medicine. Many people who dislike the idea of taking modern drugs follow naturopathy.

Among the most commonly practiced forms of alternative (or fringe) medicine are homeopathy and osteopathy. Homeopathy is a system invented by Samuel Hahnemann, a German doctor, in the 1700s. It is based on the idea that "like cures like," that is, that the cure of a disease can be brought about by drugs that can produce in a healthy person symptoms like those of the disease to be treated.

Medical research has produced drugs to cure a vast number of diseases.

For example, white arsenic is used to cure stomach upsets due to food poisoning. The homeopathic doctor takes into account the whole body and state of mind of the patient, not just the immediate problem. But homeopathy is concerned with symptoms rather than the causes or processes of a disease.

Osteopathy is a system of healing based on the belief that the body will cure itself of disease, given the opportunity. The usual obstacle to this process is supposed to be the displacement of one or more bones, which affects the blood supply to nearby organs. If the bones are put back in place, the body is free to cure itself. Osteopathy was founded in the 1800s by Andrew Still, an American doctor. Most modern practitioners regard osteopathy as an addition to conventional medicine rather than an alternative to it.

Chiropractic is a similar healing system in which mainly the bones of the spine are manipulated.

Chinese medicine has been practiced for over 5,000 years, and is based on ideas totally different from those of Western medicine. According to Chinese tradition, the body is controlled by life-giving energy, or Chi, which consists of two opposing, invisible essences – Yang and Yin. They are stored in the body in invisible burning spaces, and are transported around the body along twelve lines, or meridians. Disease is due to a disturbance of the balance between Yang and Yin. Chinese medicine relies heavily on

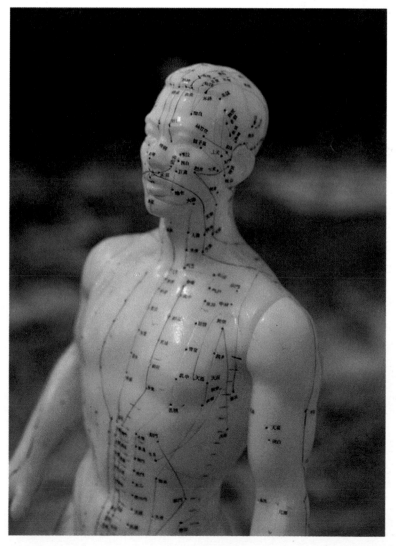

This picture shows a figure with the meridians used by acupuncturists marked upon it.

the use of acupuncture, in which needles are inserted into the body at points along the meridians to restore the balance.

Acupuncture can be used to relieve pain, for example, during operations. Western scientists accept that acupuncture is effective, and are researching how it works but, as yet, the Western world is reluctant to commit itself to a form of medicine that remains largely unexplained. At the same time, some Chinese acupuncturists are beginning to use Western technology. Electro-acupuncture, in which tiny electric currents are fed into the needles, has become common in some treatments. Sometimes fine laser beams are used instead of needles. Modern Chinese doctors learn both Western medical techniques and traditional Chinese medicine.

Scientists are now able to alter the structure of a cell, and so produce different characteristics. Here is a cell magnified many thousands of times.

Below *Electro-acupuncture is used successfully in China as a painkiller during operations. This patient was conscious throughout an operation on his thyroid gland.*

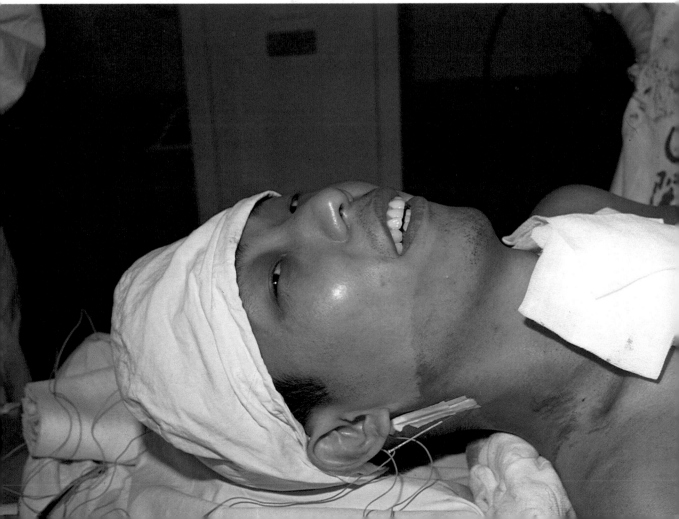

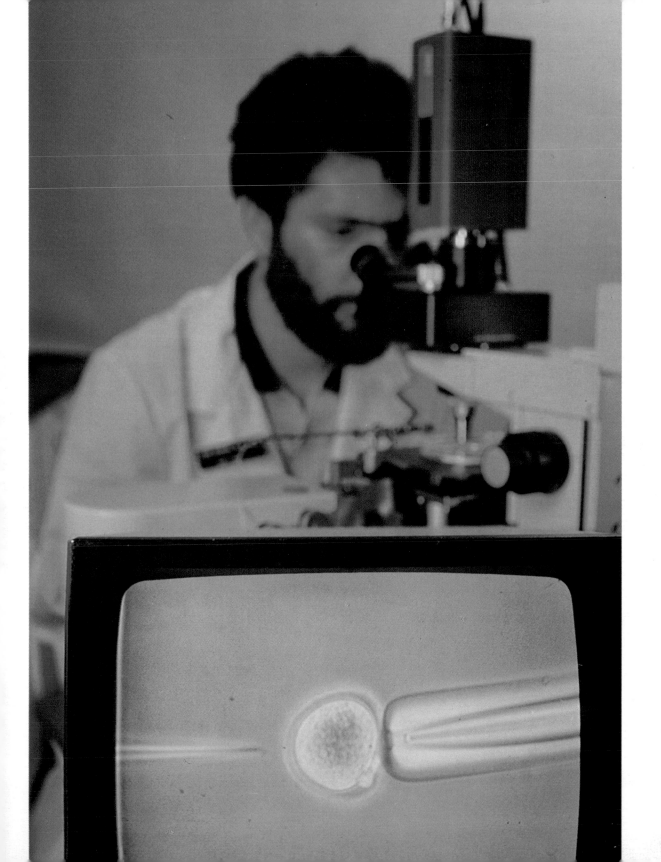

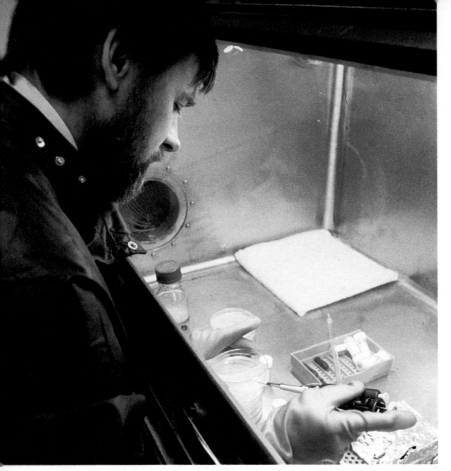

Scientist at a genetic engineering laboratory removes a virus culture from a small dish, using an automatic pipette.

The frontiers of modern medicine

The boundaries of medical knowledge and expertise are constantly being extended. But as a result we are increasingly being faced with the problem of deciding what is beneficial to the human race and what is harmful or unacceptable. For example, in recent years, genetic engineers have begun to perfect the art of altering the characteristics of living organisms. Inside the nuclei of living cells are thread-like structures known as chromosomes. A chromosome consists of a row of units called genes, each of which controls a different characteristic of the organism. Until recently it was thought that these characteristics could not be deliberately altered except by bombarding cells with radiation or chemicals that alter genes at random. But genetic engineering has changed all that. It is now possible chemically to "cut out" pieces of gene from a cell belonging to one organism, and transfer them to a cell belonging to another organism.

Genetic engineers have succeeded in creating a bacterium capable of producing appreciable amounts of human interferon. Vaccines and enzymes that can be used to make semi-synthetic antibiotic drugs have also been made in this way. Genetic engineering experiments are not restricted to microorganisms. Already, it is possible to transfer genes between plants and even mammals, including humans. Some of this work will be greatly beneficial, for example, in improving food crops and in treating disease. But it is possible to envisage experiments that would be generally regarded as unacceptable or dangerous.

Another modern technique enables women suffering from some forms of infertility to have babies. The technique is scientifically known as "in vitro" ("in glass") fertilization. The babies produced are often called "test-tube babies," but this term is not accurate, as test tubes are not even used in the process. Doctors remove a few eggs from a woman and fertilize them outside the body with sperm from her partner. Soon after the eggs start to develop into embryos, some are replaced in the mother's womb, where at least one usually develops in the normal way.

The fertility drug enabled Mr. and Mrs. Walton to have children – they produced six daughters in one confinement!

This in itself is not generally thought to be wrong or undesirable. But embryos often remain unused. Recently there has been much debate about how much research scientists should be allowed to carry out on such embryos.

Another problem that remains unsolved is the use of animals in medical experiments. Many people believe that we are justified in producing and testing new drugs and techniques in this way; other people strongly disagree.

Even death can raise difficulties. After an accident, it is now possible to keep a patient's body alive, even though the brain is technically dead. Today, the methods used to establish brain death are accepted by most people. However, patients who have suffered brain death are often a source of healthy organs for transplant operations. Doctors may be under pressure to diagnose brain death as soon as

This monkey is being used in a scientific experiment. While it is recognized that animals are a great aid to medical research, there are many people who object to the practice on the grounds that the animals suffer unnecessarily.

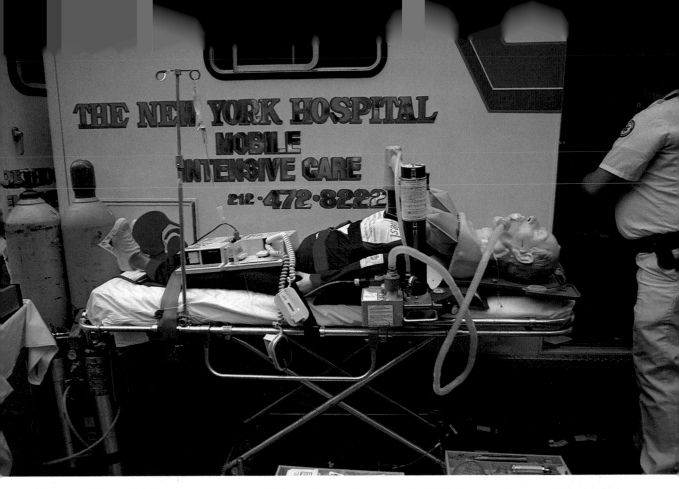

In New York, ambulances are equipped with intensive care units, which can be brought directly to the scene of an accident. This picture shows a demonstration model.

possible after it occurs, and this may cause distress to relatives.

Controversy also surrounds the use of intensive care machines to prolong the lives of dying patients. A doctor's duty is to save life rather than to hasten death. Yet to prolong life unnecessarily may cause suffering to both patients and relatives. Many people now take the view that it is reasonable to allow a patient to die with dignity.

Many problems will be resolved in the course of time. Generally, the outlook is bright for the future of medicine. Although the world may never become disease-free, people's lives will almost certainly be made easier. Perhaps death will not be permanent. Some people have even had their bodies deep frozen. Their hope is that some day scientists will find cures for the diseases that killed them, and that they will be unfrozen and restored to life and health.

Glossary

Antibiotic A substance produced by a living organism, which is used to treat a bacterial infection.

Antibody A substance produced by certain body cells in response to invasion of the body by a foreign substance, or antigen. The antibody combines chemically with the antigen, rendering it harmless.

Antiseptic A chemical that kills microorganisms without harming human tissue.

Bacteria A group of mostly one-celled microorganisms. Some cause disease.

Binocular microscope A microscope that has two eyepiece lenses, giving the viewer a three-dimensional, enlarged image of the object being examined.

Cancer An abnormal growth of some of the cells in one or more organs of the body.

Chromosomes Thread-like structures in the nucleii of living cells. They are composed of protein and the chemical DNA (deoxyribonucleic acid) and each chromosome is further divided into genes.

Gene A short length of chromosome that controls a particular feature of a living organism.

Heart-lung machine A device that can be used to bypass the body's own heart and lungs during an operation, such as open-heart surgery.

Immunity Protection given against a specific disease by inoculation or development of the body's own antibodies.

Organ A many-celled structure that forms a single functional unit, such as a kidney, a lung or the brain.

Radioactive Producing radiation in the form of particles (e.g. alpha and beta particles) or very high frequency rays.

Radiotherapy Treatment that involves exposing one or more body organs to radiation.

Tissue A group of living cells all of which have the same function.

Tumor A swelling produced by an abnormal growth of cells. A benign tumor consists of useless but harmless tissue. A malignant tumor is a cancer.

Vaccine A disease-causing virus or bacterium, changed in such a way that when it is given to a patient, it causes the body to produce antibodies against the disease without actually causing the disease itself.

Virus A minute disease-causing organism, which cannot multiply outside the tissues of a host animal or plant.

Further reading

If you would like to find out more about medicine in the future, you may like to read the following books:

Ardley, Neil. *Health and Medicine.* New York: Franklin Watts, 1982.

Brown, Paula S. *The Incredible Body Machine.* New York: Random House, 1981.

Carter, Adam. *A Day in the Life of a Medical Detective.* Mahwah, NJ: Troll Associates, 1985.

Fisher, Leonard E. *The Hospitals.* New York: Holiday House, 1980.

Jackson, Gordon. *Medicine: The Body and Healing.* New York: Franklin Watts, 1984.

McKie, Robin. *Technology: Science at Work.* New York: Franklin Watts, 1984.

Index

Acupuncture 39, 40
AIDS 34
Antibodies 27, 33
Artificial
   heart 25, 26
   heart valve 25
   kidney 26
   limbs 23
   pacemaker 24

Bacteria 27, 30, 31
Binocular microscope 18
Bioglass 24
Brain surgery 19, 21

Cancer 9, 11, 12, 30, 34
   Burkitt's lymphoma 30
   cells 32
Chemicals 9, 42
China 39, 40
Computer 11–14
   Data banks 13
Chromosomes 42

Defense system 23
Diagnosis 4, 6
Disease 4, 27, 34, 39
   bacterial 27
   parasitic 29, 36
   viral 27, 32
Donor 21, 22, 26
Drugs 31, 37
   immunosuppressive 22

Embryo 43, 44
Endoscopes 5, 6
Expert system 14

Fertilization
   in vitro 43
Gene 42
Genetic Engineering 29, 32, 42, 43
Homeopathy 37
Implant
   brain 21, 26
   cochlea 25
Immunity 27
Infection 22, 32, 34
Infertility 43
Interferon 32

Lasers 6, 19, 21
Limb death 18

Machines
   heart-lung 4, 15
   intensive care 12, 14, 15
   kidney 4
   life-support unit 4
Malaria 29
Medical experiments
   animals 23, 44
Microsurgery 18, 19
Monitor 12, 15
   cerebral function 15
   electrocardiograph 15
Monoclonal antibodies 23, 33, 34

Naturopathy 37

Optical instruments 18
Old age 21, 29, 35
Osteopathy 37, 38

Penicillin 30
Population 36

Radiation 11, 12, 42
Radiotherapy 11, 12
Rejection reaction 22
Respirator 14

Scanner
  Computerized Axial Tomography
    (CAT) 7
  gamma camera 9, 34
  ultrasound 8
  Positron Emission Tomography
    (PET) 9
  Nuclear Magnetic Resonance
    Imager (NMR) 10
Smallpox 27
Spleen cells 33
Surgery

early 5, 16
spare part 16, 23, 26

Thermal imager 7
Third World 36
Transplant 21, 22, 23, 26, 34
  heart 21
  liver 22, 26
  pancreas 22, 23

Vaccine 27, 29
Vaccination programs 27
Virus 27, 29, 32, 34

World Health Organization 27

X rays 7

Acknowledgments

The publisher would like to thank all those who provided pictures on the following pages: Antivivisectionist Society 44 (Brian Gunn); Cancer Prevention Advice 33 (Dr. Jan de Winter); Linden Artists 18, 20, 32 (Dee McClean); The MacQuitty International Photographic Collection 12, 22, 39, 40, 45; Oxfam 28, 30, 37; Rex Features 24; St. Bartholomew's Hospital 5, 7, 8 (both pictures), 9; St. Mary's Hospital 15, 23, 26; Science Photo Library cover, pages 2–3 (Will McIntyre), 4 (Russ Kinne), 6 (Alexander Tsiaras), 10 (Will McIntyre), 11 (Larry Mulvehill), 13 (Joseph Nettis), 14, 16 (Jim Stevenson), 18 (R. Stephney/M. Aumer), 29 (Martin Dohrn), 30, 36 (R. Hart Davies), 41 (Frank Morgan), 42 (John Walsh).